BIRDWATCHING

FOR THE UNDER TENS

BILL ODDIE

GEORGE
PHILIP

Picture acknowledgements
The following illustrations are reproduced by kind
permission of the Royal Society for the Protection of
Birds: RSPB/J. Markham p.7; RSPB/C.H. Gomersall pp.8
(Pheasant), 26-7, 38, 40; RSPB/P.R. Perfect pp.11
(Goldcrest), 22 (Magpie); RSPB/Roger Wilmshurst pp.11
(Little Owl), 21 (Whitethroat), 44 (Redwing), 45;
RSPB/M.K. Walker pp.11 (Kingfisher), 22 (Jay); RSPB/S. &
B.A. Craig p.13 (Lesser Black Backed Gull); RSPB/J.L.
Roberts p.20 (Blackcap); RSPB/M. Lane p.21 (Wood
Warbler); RSPB/W.S. Paton p.21 (Kestrel, Golden Eagle);
RSPB/G. Downey p.23 (Curlew)

First published by George Philip Limited,
59 Grosvenor Street, London W1X 9DA

Text © Bill Oddie 1991
Unless otherwise credited, all illustrations copyright
Bill Oddie 1991

British Library Cataloguing in Publication Data

Oddie, Bill *1941–*
    Birdwatching for the under tens.
    1. Birds
    598.07234

ISBN 0-540-01244-0

Page design Gwyn Lewis
Printed in Hong Kong

CONTENTS

1 BEFORE WE START

First of all I'm going to ask you a question. Are you REALLY interested in birds? Go on ask yourself. Is the answer 'Yes, I really, really am'? Great. Now I want you to go up to your parents and tell them: 'Mum and dad I am REALLY interested in birds.' Don't let them just say: 'Oh that's nice dear' and walk away or go back to reading the paper. Hand them this book (which they may have bought for you but probably haven't even looked at themselves!) and ask them (nicely) to read the rest of this page. You can read it too, but it's really . . .

A Message to parents . . . from Bill Oddie

Dear mum or dad
(I hope you don't mind me calling you that even though you're not MY mum or dad), your son or daughter is REALLY interested in birds (you probably know this). I am delighted, and you should be too. Birdwatching is a brilliant hobby for a youngster. Better still, it can become an interest for life. Please encourage your son or daughter as much as you can. Here are a few ways in which you can help:

MONEY Obviously if your child IS really keen he or she will prove it by saving up pocket money for bird books, magazines and so on, but there are just a few vital things that will be too expensive (unless you've just upped the pocket money an awful lot). Most important is a decent pair of binoculars – the ideal birthday or Christmas present for the budding birder. A telescope would be a REAL treat (see chapter 18). You could also help with bird club subscriptions and outings, and bird food and feeders for the garden. Buy wisely (there's more advice in this book, maybe you should read it too, actually).

TRAVEL If you have a car (and the time!) give your child a lift to and from the best birdwatching spots (more about them later too). Consider arranging family holidays in places that are also good for birds (they'll almost certainly be good for holidays too).

ENCOURAGEMENT Most important of all. Young people take their hobbies very seriously. They learn fast and they enjoy sharing their knowledge. I'm willing to bet that most kids today know a lot more about the environment and wildlife than their parents do. It's a good thing for the future of the world but it's also a bad thing because it's the adults who are in charge! So, the message is please LISTEN to your children and SHARE their enthusiasm. You'll learn a lot and you may well become a birdwatcher yourself.

Of course you may already BE a birdwatcher, in which case I hope you agree with what I've been saying to other parents. Pass it on!

Yours . . .

This is a YOC group. Do you know what those initials mean? Keep reading and you'll soon find out.

Right, how did mum or dad take it? Did they say: 'We'll see . . . we'll see', or 'It's up to you to show us you really ARE interested'. OK. That's fair enough. Now it's up to ME to write an interesting book!

Wild birds often join their tame cousins on the park lake. Look at their legs – do they have a ring on them? If not, they have flown in for a free feed.

2 HOW DID I START?

Me – a long time ago – looking ever so innocent. But was I?

I am often asked how and when I started bird-watching. I'll tell you. When I was a little boy I lived in a town called Rochdale, which is in Lancashire, in the North of England. It was definitely NOT the countryside. Our house was one of a long row. We had no garden, just a little yard with a patch of mud in it, which I suppose was meant to be a flower-bed. Our street had a big factory at one end, a main road at the other, and more houses opposite. There was hardly any greenery, except for a rather scruffy hedge that was all there was between our front door and the pavement. It really was not the sort of place where you'd expect to see many birds, and I didn't! Until one day – I was aged six I think – I was scrabbling around under the hedge looking for a lost ball, when I began to get the feeling that I was being watched. I was. There above me was a pair of beady little eyes peering over the side of a neat little nest. I never did find the ball, but I had found something much more interesting.

I showed the nest to my dad and asked him what the bird was. He had no idea. I don't think he had ever looked at a bird before. But he DID go out and buy me the only bird book you could get in those days (over 40 years ago!). It was *The Observer's Book of Birds*. I began to look through it to try and find my bird. I didn't have much to go on. All I knew was it had a little brown head (a bit like a sparrow) and it nested in a hedge. Then I turned the page and there was a picture of a little brown bird called a Hedge Sparrow (or Dunnock). Surely this was what it HAD to be.

I rushed outside and dived under the hedge to get a better look, which of course frightened the bird off the nest. Oh flip! Then it struck me. I wondered if there was anything IN the nest. I reached up and felt inside. Yes, eggs, four of them. I lifted one out and looked at it. It was a beautiful greeny blue colour. I put it back, rushed back into the house and pestered my dad to buy me another book, *The Observer's Book of Birds' Eggs*. And there it was: 'Hedge Sparrow. Eggs: Turquoise blue. Usually four.' And so began my life as a birdwatcher. Unfortunately, I also began a life of crime! I went back to the Dunnock's nest and did something really WRONG. I took an egg.

I am going to confess something to you now. I'd rather you didn't spread it around if you don't mind. And I want you to promise me that you will never ever be what I was when I was a schoolboy. I was an egg collector. To be honest, so were many of my friends. I am afraid it was one of those things that naughty school-boys almost had to do, like scrumping apples, nicking the wood from the rival gang's bonfire or pulling girls' pigtails. We did have 'rules'

A week later I was surprised to find a speckled egg among the blue ones. The Dunnocks were even more surprised when it hatched into a baby Cuckoo, which soon grew much bigger than them.

– like only taking one egg – but it really was an awful thing to do and I am pretty ashamed of it. Fortunately, I really do believe that kids today are much less destructive and much more aware about wildlife. I know for a fact that schoolboy egg collecting is almost unheard of now. What is pretty amazing, though, is that adults stealing eggs – especially of rare birds – is still a terrible problem. It is illegal and people can be fined a lot of money if they are caught, but they still do it. Well, it only goes to show that many grown up men (and it always is men, not women) are a lot more childish, selfish and destructive than young people.

3 WHY BIRDWATCHING?

I am happy to say that I wasn't a juvenile delinquent for long and, as it happens, the birds got their own back on me. One day I was watching Willow Warblers feeding their young on the edge of our local golf course, when I suddenly realized I was almost sitting in a large nest. Hidden in the grass, dangerously close to my bum, were about a dozen eggs, golden brown and almost as big as a hen's. I'd nearly squashed a Pheasant's nest. Since there were so many, I broke my 'one egg' rule and took two. I noticed that the eggs were cold and damp, and I suspected that they had been abandoned. Maybe the Pheasant had been shot by a poacher (or hit by a golf ball). Maybe the eggs had been there for ages. I was about to find out.

I took them home, made a little hole in each end, and tried to blow out the yolk, which you have to do otherwise the egg will eventually go bad. Too late. I realized that these eggs already WERE bad. They smelled awful, and the inside was all gooey. No way could I blow them. So I did a REALLY stupid thing. I sucked! If they smelled bad, they tasted worse! By taking little dollops of yucky yolk inside my mouth and spitting them out, I managed to clean out the two eggs. I then labelled them, placed them carefully in my collection and threw up all over it! I was sick for a week. I never took another egg.

Of course the reason you mustn't take birds' eggs is NOT because it can make you sick, but because it is WRONG! It is also nothing like as interesting as real birdwatching. By the age of eight or nine, I WAS a real birdwatcher. My dad was brilliant. Although he had no interest in birds himself, not only did he help me buy new bird books when they came out, but one

Fairy Terns are my favourite bird in the world. Unfortunately, they only live on tropical islands – not in Britain.

A Male Pheasant. The female is dull brown for camouflage on the nest. It seems terrible that some people enjoy shooting such a beautiful bird.

This baby Tropic Bird was photographed on the Seychelles in the Indian Ocean.

Above If you've only seen Pelicans in zoos, it is surprising to find that in the wild they often nest at the top of really tall trees.
Left The Lilac Breasted Roller from Africa is so called because of its lilac breast and its peculiar tumbling, or rolling, flight.

Christmas my 'big present' was an excellent pair of binoculars, which I continued to use until someone stole them many years later. He also helped me by giving me a lift to and from the local reservoir each Sunday (and I probably helped him by leaving him to enjoy a peaceful weekend!) and we went on holidays to some superb birdy areas like the Norfolk Broads and South Devon. I have been bird-watching for over 40 years – I am now 50 – and I am as keen as ever. I have travelled all over the world, looking for albatrosses in New Zealand or birds of paradise in the jungles of New Guinea. And yet I still get as much pleasure from seeing birds in my garden. Bird-watching can take you anywhere because there are birds everywhere. And if you start now when you are young you will have an interest for the rest of your life.

You'll also make some really good friends. In fact when I was a little boy, birdwatchers were sometimes thought of as a bit strange. Being an egg collector was OK for a while, yes, but a birdwatcher – must be bit of a weirdo! For several years I had to do most of my bird-watching on my own and I didn't bother to dis-cuss it with most of my schoolfriends because they didn't really understand. I shall never forget the relief when I moved to a new school when I was thirteen and discovered that they had a small 'bird club' where I met a few other boys (it was a boys-only school) with whom I could share my interest. In fact, it's often a good idea to go birdwatching with a friend.

Nowadays, things are much better. There are far more birdwatchers – of all ages – and it is far easier to learn. There are far more books and magazines about birds, and there are wonderful societies, like the Royal Society for the Protection of Birds (the RSPB) which has a special young people's section (the Young Ornithologists Club, the YOC) that simply did not exist when I was a lad. There are also far more bird reserves where it is easier to see birds. The only sad thing is, there are definitely NOT far more birds. Birds – like so many types of wildlife – are threatened by all sorts of problems. On the other hand, this means that whilst 40 years ago it might have been thought a bit weird to care about birds, nowadays it would be thought weird NOT to care. YOU won't be alone.

9

4 WHY BIRDS?

Another question I am often asked is: why do I prefer watching birds to say flowers, animals or insects? My answer is that actually I am interested in all kinds of wildlife, but I have to admit I do find birds rather special. Why? Well, for a start, they are easier to see! Animals are often very shy and insects are very small. Wild flowers are very beautiful – and fairly easy to watch I suppose – but, to be honest, they don't DO much! (I hope David Bellamy does not read this!) There are birds though that can DO just about everything: walk, run, hop, swim, dive, and, most impressive of all, fly. What's more, they can look fierce or funny, ugly or beautiful, tiny or enormous.

The truth is, it is fun just to WATCH a bird, even if you don't know what it is called, but I think most people like to be able to put a name to what they are seeing. I know that is the question I get asked most: 'What's this bird?' I get drawings (often really squiggly ones!) photos (often fuzzy) and descriptions (often totally baffling) of 'mystery' birds that people cannot put a name to.

Sometimes I can help and sometimes all I can do is suggest they look carefully through a good field guide to British birds (see chapter 7). The trouble is that there are so many different birds to choose from (there are at least 250 fairly common types in Britain and nearer 500 on the British list overall). People can easily get a bit boggled. Sometimes it puts them off becoming a birdwatcher. They say things like: 'Oh I could NEVER learn to recognize all those different kinds'. Maybe that is what you are thinking. Well, my answer is DON'T PANIC. It's not hard, it's fun. For a start, let's keep it simple.

Kingfisher. You usually just see them zipping past you along a stream or river. They can look blue or orange, depending on how the light catches them.

Grey Heron. They often nest in trees by lakes or reservoirs in quite built-up areas, so it's not unusual to see them flying over the middle of town.

Little Owl. That is its name, not just a description, although it is the smallest British Owl. It doesn't 'hoot', but makes a mewing call like a loud kitten.

Mute Swan. 'Mute' means silent, but in fact Mute Swans do wheeze and grunt and, in flight, their wings 'whistle'. This one is a young bird, and has not yet turned white (the so-called 'ugly duckling' of the story).

Puffins. Many people's favourite bird. They nest on the tops of sea cliffs in burrows, often in old rabbit holes.

Gulls. Birdwatchers never talk about 'seagulls'. In fact, there are lots of different kinds.

Goldcrest. This is a good name, because it has got a little gold crest on its head. It is Britain's smallest bird, at only 9 cms long. Look out for them in fir trees.

Swallows. These two are resting on the English south coast having just flown all the way from Africa. How do they find their way? I'll talk more about migration in later chapters.

All of these are British birds.

Kingfisher

Grey Heron

Little Owl

Mute Swan

Puffins

Gulls

Goldcrest

Swallows

5 BIRDS AT HOME

HOUSE MARTIN

NOTE WHITE RUMP

" SCREECHING FLOCKS ... ARRIVE EARLY MAY.

SWIFT

WINGS MAKE 'CLAPPING' NOISE..

FLOCKS IN AUTUMN & WINTER

STARLING
SONG OFTEN MIMICS OTHER BIRDS

WOOD PIGEON

GARDEN SKETCH BOOK ....

"KEEP LOOKING UP!" Bill Oddie.

'I never get anything but sparrows in my garden.' It seems like every week that someone says that to me. It is never true. Even my muddy backyard in Rochdale would have been visited by at least half a dozen species in a week – House and Hedge Sparrows, Starlings, Robins, Blackbirds and Song Thrushes, there's six already – and if I had kept a list of everything I saw on my way to and from school I bet it would have been well over 30 for the year. Don't believe me? Have a go for yourself. One of the secrets is to keep looking up. Even in the middle of a busy city there are always birds flying over. In winter there will be flocks of gulls going to roost at a reservoir or feed on a rubbish dump (and there are four fairly common species of gulls). They often sit out on school playing fields. Next time you see a flock, have a good look at them and you'll realize they are not all the same.

In summer there will be Swifts screeching and House Martins chirrupping overhead. That is another good tip: keep using your ears. A horrible squawk may come from a Heron flying over town, looking absolutely enormous, or a clapping sound may be made by the wings of a flock of Wood Pigeons. I've even heard the calls of wild geese and swans right over my house in the middle of London. It really is a good idea to start keeping lists. How many species do you see in a year, or even a month or day, and where? It makes you look at every bird and try to identify it, but don't get put off if you cannot name them all. What you will realize is that you are seeing far more species than you first expected.

Right **Herring Gull**. The most numerous of the big gulls. The one you'll definitely see at the seaside, although they can also occur inland. This is an adult. Younger birds have all sorts of blotchy browner plumages.

12

Black headed Gull. The commonest gull inland. These fairly small gulls lose the black hood in winter, when they visit parks, gardens and fields and even follow the plough on farmland.

Common Gull. Despite its name it is not all that common, but look out for them among flocks of Black Headeds. They are just a little bigger.

Lesser Black Backed Gull. It is almost as big as a Herring Gull, and has a 'big brother' (not so common and seen only at the coast) called – guess what – the Great Black Backed Gull.

The easiest and best place to start watching and recognizing birds and keeping your first list is in your garden, or if you haven't got a garden – like me when I was a little lad – in your yard or from your house or flat windows. You could call it your 'Home list'. You don't even need binoculars for this kind of birdwatching, especially if you attract birds closer by putting up nest boxes and putting out water and food.

These days there are all kinds of feeders and tables that you can buy. Don't worry if you cannot afford them. The truth is that the birds will be perfectly happy if you scatter seed and crumbs on the ground or on a garden wall, and Blue Tits will be as content with a dangling bag of peanuts or half a coconut as with some fancy plastic contraption that gets chewed to pieces by Grey Squirrels. Squirrels are lovely but they do pinch the nuts, so if you buy a feeder do make sure it is a really tough one with a wire grille.

The main thing about putting out food is to make sure it is at different levels to suit different birds because, as you'll soon notice, different species feed in different ways. You won't see Robins or Blackbirds dangling on the nutbags. They like pecking around on the floor, and in fact if they can find worms and grubs that's what they prefer. Song Thrushes

Song Thrush

THRUSHES

The Song Thrush has a speckled breast – just like a thrush ought to have – but the Robin is much the same shape, only smaller. The white bird could be a real puzzler, but its shape gives it away. It is an albino Blackbird, and Blackbirds are also in the thrush family.

Above **Robin**   *Below* **Blackbird**

Blue Tit

Coal Tit

Great Tit

TITS

An easy family to study. All you have to do is put out nuts in the yard or garden and I'll almost guarantee that you will see these three species. There are, though, other tit species that won't come to the feeder.

love snails, which they break open on stones or rocks. If you find a pile of broken shells it is a thrush's 'anvil'. In fact Robins, thrushes and Blackbirds all belong to the same family. Notice they all have rather thin pointed beaks. Now look at the House Sparrows' beaks and you'll see that they are short and stubby, specially suited to cracking open seeds, whilst the tits have fine little beaks with which they can catch tiny insects as well as nibble nuts.

So, here are the rules for home bird-watching: see how many different species there are, study how they feed and notice their beak shapes. You'll find it's really important when you come to putting a name to the birds.

House Sparrow

Chaffinch

SEED EATERS

These two species are among the commonest birds in Britain, but there are lots of other seed eaters, including various finches and buntings. They come in all sorts of colours but they ALL have those stubby little beaks.

7 FIELD GUIDES

Big word 'identification'. Do you know what it means? (Little pause whilst you have a think.) It means being able to put a name to a bird (or anything else) that you see. So if you see a little brown bird with a red breast and you say: 'That's a Robin', you have identified it. (Sorry if you knew this already, and sorry if this sounds like an English lesson!) It is easy to identify a Robin or a Blackbird or a House Sparrow because everybody knows them well. But if you see a bird you've never seen before how do you identify it? Answer: you look it up in a book. But which book? Not THIS book. What you need is an identification book. They are called 'field guides', but they are not guides to fields. (I'm sure you could identify a field: it's a big green thing!) Field guides help you identify all kinds of wildlife. So, you can get guides to wild flowers, butterflies and other insects, animals or, of course, birds. A good field guide is the one book that every birdwatcher MUST have.

Maybe you are going to save up for one yourself or maybe it will be a present from your parents. Either way I want to help you make sure you don't waste your money by buying a 'bad' field guide. The trouble is there are lots of books in the shops that you may THINK look like field guides but which are not. They may look great, full of glossy photos or paintings and they may be called something like *The World of Birds*, *Birds of the World* or just

Birds, but though they are lovely to look at, they won't really help you to identify what you see. There are also books that tell you about birdwatching – like this one – but they aren't field guides either.

So how do you identify a field guide? Well, for a start, many of them are actually called something like *A Field Guide* or *Guide . . . to Birds of Britain* (and possibly Europe). So start by looking at those. You may find that some of them have photographs of the birds instead of paintings. This may seem better but in fact it isn't necessarily so, because a good artist can show a bird more clearly than most photographs. Here are some rules to follow when choosing your field guide.

1. It should be small enough to put into a large pocket or bag. But not too tiny because
2. It should have a full selection of all but the rarest British birds in it, so that means over 250 species.
3. There should be several illustrations of most of the species (I'll tell you why in a minute). Check this by looking at a few pages and you should see that drawings are labelled things like 'male' and 'female', 'adult', 'juvenile', 'summer', 'winter' and so on. Don't worry if you are not quite sure what it all means or if it even seems a bit confusing. You will be more confused if you buy a field guide that only has one picture of each species (and I promise I WILL tell you why . . . in a minute).
4. Alongside the pictures should be lots of information on how to identify the bird: this should include descriptions of its calls and songs and information on its habits and where it lives (its habitat). There should also be maps showing which parts of the country it is found in and at which times of the year.

I have given a list of five of the best field guides and you won't go wrong if you choose one of these. (Of course there may be new ones out already, but make sure you check the 'rules' before you or your parents buy one.)

The RSPB Book of British Birds, by Holden, Sharrock and Burn (published by Macmillan)
The Mitchell Beazley Birdwatcher's Pocket Guide, by Peter Hayman (Mitchell Beazley)
The Shell Guide to the Birds of Britain and Ireland, by Ferguson-Lees, Willis and Sharrock (Michael Joseph)
Kingfisher Field Guide to the Birds of Britain and Europe, by Gooders and Harris (Kingfisher)
A Field Guide to the Birds of Britain and Europe, by Peterson, Mountfort and Hollom (Collins)

I promised I'd explain, so I will. The thing is that many species of birds do not always look the same. Sounds like a riddle? OK, here's another one. When does a Robin 'redbreast' NOT have a red breast? Answer: when it is a baby, because young Robins are speckly brown all over. And when is a Blackbird NOT a black bird? Answer: when it is a female, because a male Blackbird is black but a female

Black Headed Gull. 1 Summer adult. **1a** Summer adult in flight. **2** Winter Adult. **3** Juvenile. **4** First winter. **4a** First winter in flight.

is brown. And here's another one. There is a bird called a Black-headed Gull. It's a good name because it has got a black head (sometimes), BUT when is a Black-headed Gull NOT a black-headed gull? Answer: in the winter. Are you beginning to understand why your field guide should have so many pictures? Each species should be shown in all its different plumages, not just the prettiest, which are usually the male's (it's different in the bird world you see). Males and females often look very different, so do young birds and adults, and some species look much more colourful during the summer than they do in winter.

How do birds actually change the way they look? By changing their feathers, just as you or I might change our clothes. Except that birds don't do it quite so often! In most cases birds change their plumage once or twice a year. This is called 'moulting'. It is a slow process. They don't just suddenly lose all their feathers so that they look like plucked chickens! With small birds, the body feathers usually begin dropping out in late summer (after they have reared their young), then they grow nice new feathers on the body. Then their wing and tail feathers drop out one by one and new ones grow. Why do you think they don't lose all their wing feathers at the same time? That's right they would not be able to fly. Actually this is exactly what DOES happen to some birds, especially ducks and geese. When they are moulting sometimes their wings become almost useless and all they can do is flap and flutter and hardly get off the ground. Fortunately for the ducks they can swim away from danger or stay out on an island safe from foxes and the like.

On the rest of this page are a few species in different plumages – as you should see them in the field guide – just to show you HOW different they can look.

Goldfinch. 1 Adult. **2** Juvenile.

Reed Bunting. 1 Male ♂. **1a** Male ♂ in winter. **2** Female ♀.

Shoveler. 1 Male ♂. **1a** Male ♂ in partial eclipse (moult). **2** Female ♀.

9   FAMILIES

O K, let's say you have bought your field guide (or you are going to). I am sure if you glance through it the one thing you'll be amazed at is just how many different kinds of birds there are to be seen in Britain (or anywhere else). It's exciting. You may think: 'Oh I'll never see half of those', but if you become a birdwatcher I promise you that you soon will. In some really good places it is possible to see well over a hundred different kinds in a day. So that's encouraging isn't it? On the other hand, maybe you feel a bit worried that there are so many pictures of so many birds that you'll never be able to sort it all out. Please don't worry. I'll help you learn how to use your field guide and very, very soon you will be able to help yourself. I promise!

Start by just skimming right through the book, having a bit of a look at each page and noticing how many birds or kinds of birds you DO recognize. I think you'll be pleasantly surprised. Then I want you to notice something else. The birds are all grouped in what are called 'families'. All field guides should show the birds in the same order. On the first page there will be some sleek-looking water birds called 'divers'; then come the grebes (maybe you'll recognize the first one here: the Great Crested Grebe), then on through the ducks and geese; birds of prey, and so on ... right

Above **Wood Warbler**   *Below* **Blackcap**

Whitethroat

This is a hard family to identify – many of them are just 'little brown birds' – but they all have dainty insect eaters' beaks. They tend to flit around in trees, bushes or reeds, rather than hop on the floor. They also have distinctive songs that you should get to know. Mind you, they don't all 'warble', some of them 'scratch' and 'squeak'!

WARBLERS

through to the last pages of sparrows and other seed-eating birds. (Do you remember them from the garden bird table?)

When you are out birdwatching and you see a bird that you can't identify, the first thing you should try to do is to decide which family it belongs to. Then when it comes to looking for it in the field guide later you will be able to turn to the right few pages rather than having to look right through the whole book each time you see a bird you don't know.

So how do you decide about the family? Remember those birds in your garden? Remember that I said Robins and Blackbirds both belonged to the thrush family and that they both had thin pointed beaks. So do all members of the thrush family. And I said that all the tits have little short, thin beaks, and the seed-eaters little stubby ones. Well THAT'S the key thing to notice: the birds' beaks. Generally speaking all birds in a certain family feed in a similar way and that means they will all have similar kinds of beaks. It doesn't mean they'll look EXACTLY the same – a big thrush will have a big beak and a little one a little beak – but they ARE more or less the same shape.

I can only show a few bird families in a little book like this. You look through your field guide to see how many there are.

Kestrel

'Raptors' is a scientific name for 'birds of prey'. This family includes hawks, falcons, buzzards, eagles and vultures (although we don't get them in Britain). There are small raptors and huge ones, all with hooked beaks for tearing meat.

Above **Golden Eagle**   *Below* **Osprey**

RAPTORS

Above **Crow**   *Below* **Magpie**

Jay

We all know a Crow is black, and so are Rooks, but did you know that the beautifully coloured Jay is also a 'crow'? So is the Magpie. Crows are perhaps the most intelligent of all birds, but they are NOT known for their songs – they all just 'caw', 'chatter' or 'screech'.

CROWS

Above **Common Tern**   *Below* **Little Tern**

Arctic Tern

It is not difficult to see that these are related. Terns look like small graceful gulls. Common Terns often nest on inland reservoirs or gravel pits, especially if 'rafts' are provided for them.

TERNS

Avocet

Ringed Plover

Curlew

Dunlin

Above Snipe   *Below* Oystercatcher

This is a big family which includes birds that hardly look related at all! They are called 'waders' because they generally feed on the sandy shore or on muddy estuaries. The length and shape of their beaks varies depending on what kind of food they prefer. For example, the Ringed Plover's stubby little beak is perfect for picking food off the surface, while the Curlew can probe right down in the soft mud. Because they come in all these wonderful different shapes and sizes, several species of wader can share the same habitat without competing for food.

WADERS

10 BINOCULARS

So, you've bought your field guide and had a look through it. There is obviously a lot to see and a lot to learn. Instead of putting you off it has got you really excited about the whole thing. You've definitely decided, you really do want to become a birdwatcher. OK this is the time to go back to mum and dad and convince them that you are serious and that you really do need a pair of binoculars to do it properly.

It's true that you can enjoy birds in the garden or the park without binoculars but if you want to get out and see all those wonderful waders and wildfowl and identify those little warblers and buntings which will be farther away then your eyes are going to need a bit of help! So, here are the rules for persuading parents that they ought to help you buy a pair of binoculars.

1. You must convince them that you really ARE serious (oh, you've done that. Good).
2. Assure them that binoculars are probably not as expensive as they THINK.
3. Tell them that, if they buy carefully, a good pair will last for years.
4. Promise that mum or dad can use them too (even if it's only when they go racing or to the theatre!).
5. Lastly tell them to read this chapter and take my advice so that they won't waste their money by buying a duff pair!

There are several different species on this shoreline. You could use a magnifying glass to identify them here, but 'in the field' you would definitely need binoculars.

So, parents, this bit is for you too.

Please DON'T buy binoculars on 'special offer' as advertised in the newspaper. Also please DON'T buy them from the local chemist or camera shop, unless you happen to know that it is run by a birdwatcher. These days there are lots of dealers who specialize in optical equipment (binoculars, telescopes, cameras) specially for birdwatching. They advertise in such magazines as *Birdwatching* or BBC *Wildlife* which are available at the newsagent. Or if anyone in the family belongs to the RSPB, their magazine will also have information about binoculars. The best thing of all is if you can visit the showroom, take advice from the expert and try out the binoculars. Often you will be able to have them on approval for a week or two and if they don't suit you, you can exchange them. If you can't get to the showroom, ring up the dealer and let him or her advise you about what is best for a youngster, at the price you want to pay.

The binoculars should magnify between seven and ten times. Probably for a youngster

Don't be confused by the huge choice in the adverts. It is better to take an expert's advice.

'×8' would be best. Make sure they are not too big (or you will get neckache!) or too small. Tiny little binoculars seem like a great idea – and there ARE some pretty good ones – but the problem is that they don't show as big an area (it's called the 'field of view') and it can be hard to follow a moving bird. There is no point in my recommending actual makes of binoculars here because there are so many and at very different prices. Also it's MUCH better if you call or go and see that specialist dealer I mentioned, PLEASE.

When you get your new binoculars (let's hope), also get a rainguard, which will cover the eyepieces in wet weather. Shorten the strap so they hang comfortably on your chest. And when you are out birdwatching, keep them round your neck at ALL times. DON'T carry them in the case. By the time you've got them out the bird will have flown away!

11 WHAT ELSE DO YOU NEED?

A field guide and binoculars are the two really important things. You have to get used to using them both. I'll go back to the field guide later but just a last word on those new binoculars. At first they may feel a bit 'funny'. It's only because you're not used to seeing things eight times bigger than normal. You may also have trouble 'finding' the birds in the binoculars at first. Just be patient and practise. The rule is: spot the bird with your naked eyes, THEN look at it through binoculars. You will very soon get the idea and I promise you will be thrilled by the amazing close-up views. Just try looking at a sparrow or a Blue Tit through binoculars, notice how neat and yet complicated all the feathers are and how many shades of colour there are.

If you go to the specialist you may also see telescopes. Telescopes give you a REAL close-up view – between twenty and 50 times – but

Three views of a pack of waders: above, with the naked eye; right, through binoculars; and far right – for a real close-up – through a telescope.

they are much harder to use for normal bird-watching. For a start you need to put them on a tripod to keep them steady and you certainly can't follow a fast-flying bird through a telescope. Serious birdwatchers DO usually buy a telescope eventually, but I wouldn't worry about it yet. Mind you, if you get REALLY, REALLY keen, I expect you'll be back pleading with parents again! If you do want to look at telescopes the rule is the same. Please go to the specialist dealer.

Another thing you ought to think a bit about when you go out birdwatching is clothes! No, I know you're not going to forget to put on your trousers or skirt, I just mean

26

that you should make sure you don't wear a luminous anorak or a bright coloured sweater. It's quite simple. If you want to see birds you don't really want them to see you! Also make sure you are protected against bad weather. If you are going to be out all day it may well change, so YOU should be able to as well. Even if it is sunny when you set out it's still worth popping a waterproof in a bag. If it is cold and wet it may clear up and get warmer and you could boil if you are wearing a great big, thick coat. I find the best idea is to wear a few layers ... maybe a T-shirt, a sweat shirt and a light anorak. Then you can slip in and out of things as the weather changes. And if you're likely to be near mud, don't forget your wellies. Oh and don't forget to take them off when you come back in the house. Whoops, I'm beginning to sound like mum now. Sorry.

OK, so is that all you need when you are off out birdwatching? Sensible clothes, binoculars, field guide, packed lunch maybe, a bit of money. Ah yes, one more thing: a little note book and a pencil (and a sharpener might be a good idea in case it breaks). This is really important. You need a note book for two reasons. Firstly to write down all the birds you recognize and secondly to write notes about the birds you don't recognize – the ones you cannot identify. This is where birdwatching gets really fascinating.

When you are out birdwatching you'll soon find you recognize a lot of the birds you see. Then there will be some you sort of half recognize – you'll have a quick look in the field guide and find them quickly. BUT there will sometimes be a few that are really puzzling. This is when you'll need to jot down a description of the mystery bird which will help you when you look it up in the field guide.

27

12 TAKING NOTES

So what exactly do you put in your little note book (often called a field note book because you take it out into 'the field' – which just means out anywhere really – along with your field guide)?

Note the date, the place, and the weather, including the wind direction if possible. Look for a weather vane on a church which will tell you where north, south, east and west are. And remember you note where the wind is coming FROM (the way the arrow points on the vane an east wind is one coming FROM the east). (A wind blowing TO the east would be a what wind?) You should also note the time of the day you are out. You put all this information down for two reasons. Firstly, because your note book should be a kind of 'bird diary'. In fact, a lot of birdwatchers copy all their field notes – which may be a bit scribbly – neatly into a big note book later. I have over twenty volumes of bird note books going back to when

I was a boy and I often still read them and remember particularly good days and exciting birds. The second reason for noting the time, place and weather is that it might be very useful to you if you see a bird you can't identify. (I'll tell you how in a minute.)

You should then note down more or less ALL the birds you recognize on a day out. Note the species and the numbers and if you see any large flocks flying over, note the direction they are flying. Also note down any interesting 'behaviour', which simply means what the birds are doing. For example you might see Robins fighting, or swallows gathering on the telephone wires before they fly south in autumn. So that's the first reason for taking notes: keeping a bird diary.

The second reason is to take a description of birds you don't recognize. If you DO see a puzzling bird it's all too easy to either panic or get overexcited, especially if you think it

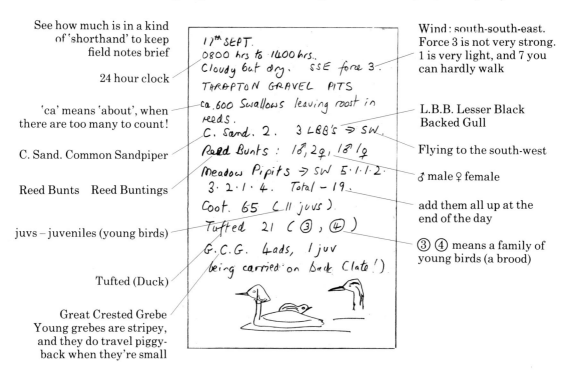

See how much is in a kind of 'shorthand' to keep field notes brief

24 hour clock

'ca' means 'about', when there are too many to count!

C. Sand. Common Sandpiper

Reed Bunts   Reed Buntings

juvs – juveniles (young birds)

Tufted (Duck)

Great Crested Grebe
Young grebes are stripey, and they do travel piggy-back when they're small

17ᵗʰ SEPT.
0800 hrs to 1400 hrs.
Cloudy but dry.   SSE force 3.
THRAPTON GRAVEL PITS
ca.600 Swallows leaving roost in reeds.
C. Sand. 2.   3 LBB's ⇒ SW.
Reed Bunts : 18, 2♀, 18/♀
Meadow Pipits ⇒ SW 5·1·1·2·
3·2·1·4.   Total – 19.
Coot. 65 (11 juvs).
Tufted 21 (③ , ④)
G.C.G. 4ads, 1 juv
being carried on back (late!)

Wind: south-south-east.
Force 3 is not very strong.
1 is very light, and 7 you can hardly walk

L.B.B. Lesser Black Backed Gull

Flying to the south-west

♂ male ♀ female

add them all up at the end of the day

③ ④ means a family of young birds (a brood)

28

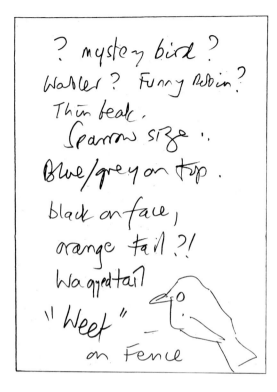

? mystery bird ?
Warbler ? Funny Robin ?
Thin beak.
Sparrow size ..
Blue/grey on top.
black on face,
orange tail ?!
Wagged tail
"Weet"
on Fence

Notice how your handwriting goes all squiggly when you're excited. This description is rather vague. Look at the next chapter to see how it should be done. . .

might be something really rare. So let's imagine you have just found a 'funny' bird and you are thinkng to yourself: 'I really don't know what this is'. Here is another little list of rules to help you.

1. DON'T immediately start searching through your field guide for minutes on end. You probably won't find the bird quickly, then you will look up and it will have flown away. Your field guide WON'T fly away, so you can always look at that later. So the first rule is to look at the bird for as long as you can.

2. Then: take notes. Pay special attention to the shape of the beak, feeding behaviour and general shape and start thinking: 'What family does this belong to?'

3. Then: note the most obvious plumage features, especially areas of colour or any markings that particularly stand out. It is a good idea to go along the bird from head to tail describing each bit in turn.

4. Listen for any song or calls and try and write them down too.

5. You should have already noted the date, place, kind of habitat, and weather.

6. Also: do a drawing. It doesn't matter if you're not very good at drawing. I think that a really awful drawing is often better than no drawing at all. It is often the quickest way to do a description because you can 'point to' the colours and markings.

What IS important, though – whether you do a description or a drawing – is that you note EXACTLY where the colours and markings are. OK over the page . . .

13 BIRDS' BITS AND PIECES

If you were describing a person you wouldn't just say 'Er, he's sort of pinkish with brown bits on his face, red above and blue lower down'. You would be more accurate and detailed: 'He has a pink face, but with rosy cheeks, dark brown hair, green eyes, red sweater over a white shirt, blue trousers and so on.' Birds don't wear clothes but they do have feathers. Different areas of feathers have names, just like our parts of the body. In fact, if we were being really scientific, many of these names are very complicated – usually in Latin – and not easy to remember. Many field guides have a page full of drawings at the front of a sort of identikit bird with all its bits and pieces marked and named. It is a good idea to

study this but perhaps not yet as it might put you off! (I know I STILL have trouble remembering all the parts.) For the moment let's keep it a bit simpler.

Here are some drawings of birds with the main areas marked on them. When you are doing a quick field sketch of a 'mystery' bird it is not a bad idea to divide it up as I have done here and note down the colours and markings in each area. I've already said you don't have to be a great artist – and it is true – but you should try to get used to doing a simple shape of several different families of birds. If you REALLY can't bring yourself to do a sketch then you should take careful notes describing each part of the bird in turn.

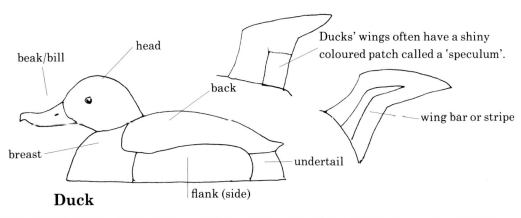

Ducks' wings often have a shiny coloured patch called a 'speculum'.

wing bar or stripe

Duck

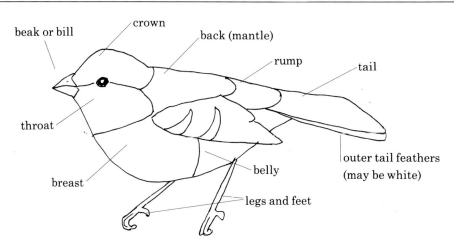

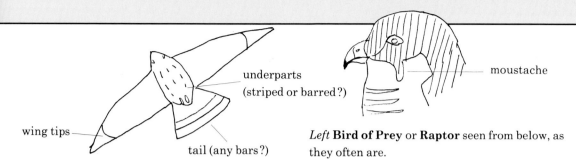

underparts (striped or barred?)

moustache

wing tips

tail (any bars?)

Left **Bird of Prey** or **Raptor** seen from below, as they often are.

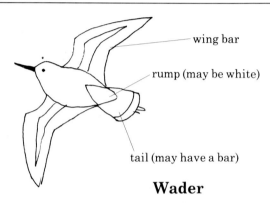

wing bar

rump (may be white)

tail (may have a bar)

Wader

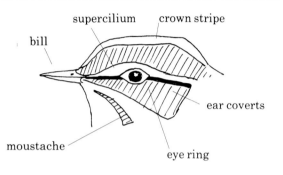

supercilium   crown stripe

bill

ear coverts

moustache

eye ring

Head pattern. This can be complicated – if you can't remember all the big names, at least look closely at where the markings are.

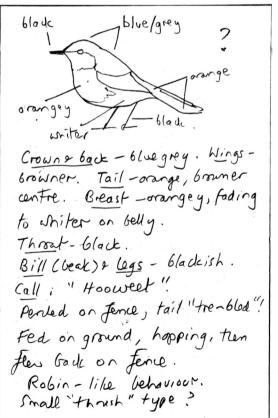

black   blue/grey   ?

orange

orangey

writer

black.

Crown & back — blue grey. Wings — browner. Tail — orange, browner centre. Breast — orangey, fading to whiter on belly.
Throat — black.
Bill (beak) & legs — blackish.
Call ; " Hooweet "!
Perched on fence, tail "trembled"!
Fed on ground, hopping, then flew back on fence.
  Robin - like behaviour.
Small "thrush" type ?

Ad. ♂ REDSTART
THRAPTON
17th SEPT.

And this is how the 'mystery' bird ended up in my 'big notebook'.

'Confusion species'. Male Golden Oriole (rare) and Green Woodpecker (common). They are members of completely different families, and you won't find them on the same page in the field guide, but they can look very similar, especially on the ground or in flight.

So now let's suppose you have seen a 'mystery' bird. You have taken a careful description and you have maybe done a little sketch. Unfortunately the bird has now flown away. Don't worry. You should have enough down in your little note book to be able to identify it.

Here is another set of rules. (Sorry if mentioning rules sounds a bit like school. Just remember these rules are definitely here to make things easier and more fun.) So, rules for looking up a mystery bird in the field guide:

1. Read your own field notes, look at your drawing and have a little think. What family do you think the bird belongs to? Hopefully you will be able to decide and will turn to a page of birds that look something like what you saw. If nothing does come to mind, have a very quick skim through the field guide till you find a page of birds that look something like yours. Remember it's the beak and general shape that decide a family.

2. Then: if the shape looks right but you can't recognize the plumage, consider if it could be a female, juvenile (young bird), is in its winter plumage or maybe actually a bird which is moulting, when some can look really tatty. It's possible that your field guide doesn't have a picture of ALL the plumages. It might just say: 'Female is similar to male but much duller' or 'Juvenile is speckled brown'.

3. If you still can't find your bird in the family you THOUGHT it belonged to, read the descriptions of some of the species that look a bit like it. You may find that the book mentions something called 'confusion species'. This means birds that look rather similar but AREN'T in the same family. It CAN happen, and it IS confusing. (That is why they are called confusion species!) So have a look at them next.

4. If you STILL can't find your bird, try going through the book saying what it definitely WASN'T! What are you left with? Anything? Well, if you STILL can't find it you've either bought the wrong field guide, the bird has escaped from a zoo, or it is something really rare. Which brings me to THE golden rule: YOU should always start off by assuming that whatever you see is fairly common. Just because you don't recognize it, it doesn't mean that it is rare. 'Puzzling birds' are more likely to be common birds in confusing plumages than real rarities. So when you are looking up a mystery bird in the book, try to resist

immediately checking out all the rarities. On the other hand, just now and then you will be lucky and you WILL find something rare. This next and final rule still applies.

5. Let's pretend now that you have 'found' your mystery bird in the book. Just ask yourself one last question: 'Should it be there?' This is why you noted the date and place. The field guide will tell you whether it is a summer or winter visitor, and the type of habitat it prefers, and the little map shows you which part of the country it occurs in. Checking these things really does help you decide if your identification is right or wrong. For example, let's say you've seen a big black bird flying over London. You thought it might be a Raven. But the book tells you Ravens live in cliffs and mountains – not towns – and the map shows they only occur on the west side of Britain. So it was more likely to have been a Crow. Or let's say you heard a bird singing at night just before Christmas. A Nightingale? No, the book tells us Nightingales only visit us in the summer. It is more likely to have been a Robin. In fact Robins often sing at night!

I know some of this may all seem a bit complicated but please don't be put off. For a start all this 'detective work' is great fun, and you'll find that most birds are quite easy to recognize. And it's brilliantly exciting when you really DO find a rarity (more about them later in chapter 21).

Wrens are very common – but they skulk in the undergrowth. If you see a Wren's head peeping out it is easy to mistake it for a little brown warbler, like the three on the right (from top to bottom) Sedge Warbler (common), Radde's Warbler (very rare), and Cetti's Warbler (quite rare). The rule is, if you think you've spotted a rare warbler, are you sure it isn't a Wren?

Two more 'confusion species' that you won't find on the same page of your field guide, the Cuckoo and the male Sparrow Hawk. They are both grey above, barred below and fly fast and low.

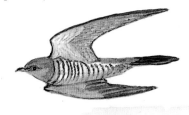

15   YOUR LOCAL PATCH

A variety of
habitats close to
each other makes
for an ideal
local patch.

As it happens, you could say that a rare bird is any bird that you have not seen before. For example if you have never seen a Raven then, to you, it is rare, even though Ravens are quite common if you go to the right place (the mountains in Wales for example). Then again if that black bird you saw flying over London really WAS a Raven, that would be rare too because Ravens aren't normally seen there. Do you see what I'm getting at?

It IS exciting to see something new and unusual. If you collect stamps or train numbers, I'm sure you will agree.

The one way of making sure you enjoy 'collecting' new birds is by regularly watching what birdwatchers call a 'local patch'. This is an area that you visit throughout the year, at all seasons, maybe several times a week. You keep a note of everything you see and a list of all the species you record. So, anything new to your list is a rarity – for your patch. It is a great way to get to know the more common birds and you'll notice – and may be surprised by – how many different birds come and go at different times of the year.

The ideal local patch has a variety of what you could call 'mini habitats'. It's especially good if it includes an area of water, which will not only attract water birds but also insects which in turn attract small insect-eating warblers and flycatchers. Fields of rough grass and weeds will appeal to the seed-eaters. Hedges will have berries for the thrushes and so on. The fact is that different habitats attract different birds so the more variety your patch has the more birds you'll see there. If you live inland, ideal local patches could be school grounds, a park, or even an area of allotments. Best of all though are gravel pits or reservoirs which may even attract birds that normally belong near the sea. If you are lucky enough to live near the coast then an estuary or headland, especially if there are woods and marshes nearby, will be a perfect patch.

When I was a boy my own local patch was a rather bleak-looking reservoir just on the outskirts of Birmingham. It was by no means countryfied and there were housing estates and roads all round it. Nevertheless, I went there week after week (day after day in the school holidays) for ten years and never got bored. I drew a careful map of the area and marked in all the different habitats and each time I paid a visit I made sure I carefully covered each one. I copied up all my notes into a big note book, and added graphs and tables

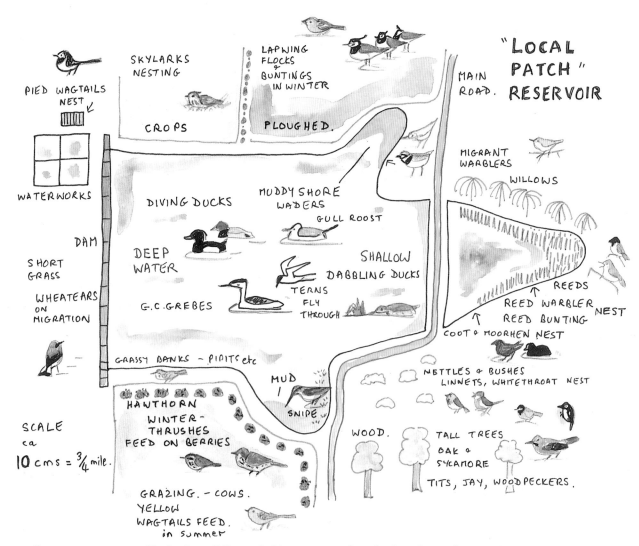

PIED WAGTAILS NEST

SKYLARKS NESTING

LAPWING FLOCKS & BUNTINGS IN WINTER

"LOCAL PATCH" RESERVOIR

MAIN ROAD

CROPS

PLOUGHED.

MIGRANT WARBLERS

WILLOWS

WATERWORKS

DIVING DUCKS

MUDDY SHORE WADERS

GULL ROOST

DAM

DEEP WATER

SHALLOW DABBLING DUCKS

SHORT GRASS

REEDS

WHEATEARS ON MIGRATION

G.C.GREBES

TERNS FLY THROUGH

REED WARBLER NEST
REED BUNTING

COOT & MOORHEN NEST

GRASSY BANKS — PIPITS etc

MUD

NETTLES & BUSHES
LINNETS, WHITETHROAT NEST

HAWTHORN WINTER-THRUSHES FEED ON BERRIES

SNIPE

WOOD.

TALL TREES OAK & SYCAMORE

SCALE
ca
10 cms = ¾ mile.

GRAZING. — COWS.
YELLOW WAGTAILS FEED.
in summer

TITS, JAY, WOODPECKERS.

Draw your own map. Notice how different habitats attract different species.

showing how the numbers of birds varied through the year and I even went to the local library and discovered old Bird Club records from the area that went back 30 years before I'd started watching it. Eventually, I wrote a sort of bird history book about the place and won the school natural history prize with it! Sorry to boast, but I was really proud of my local patch and if you start watching one, I'm sure you will be too.

I have to finish this chapter with more rules though (oh no, not again!). The one not so nice thing I remember from being a schoolboy bird-watcher is that I was forever being chased or shouted at by farmers and reservoir keepers. I was stupid. I never did really find out which bits of my patch were private. The rule is simple: always ask permission if you think an area might be private and definitely if there are any 'no trespassing' notices. If you say you are a serious birdwatcher you'll usually be given permission. If you're NOT it is probably for your own good – there may be a bull in the field, a Ministry of Defence firing range nearby, or maybe there is dangerous mud or deep water. Also always obey the country code and make sure you don't climb fences, walk in crops or leave gates open. It's all common sense and the reward is that YOU won't be shouted at or chased away!

Looking into the sun, you can see just 'black ducks'.

With the sun behind you, they are obviously male and female Mallards.

I have already said that different habitats attract different birds. It is a good rule (another one) when you are out birdwatching to keep thinking to yourself: 'What do I EXPECT to find here?' That way you'll make sure you see all there is to see and also be aware when you see something unusual. That is another kind of rarity really. I mean a Kestrel hovering over the motorway is a pretty common sight but if one dropped into your garden it would be much more exciting! The more you get out and birdwatch in different habitats the more you will learn about what to expect. Here are a few tips (I won't call them rules!) about making the most of your time out in the field.

First of all, two rules (sorry, tips) that apply wherever you are. Number one: get up early! Birds are always more active – and easier to see – feeding, flying and singing just after the sun comes up. Bushes that were alive with birds just after dawn can become completely quiet a few hours later. What is more, there will be fewer people around to disturb you and the birds. Number two: keep the sun behind you. You would never take a photograph looking into the sun: it would dazzle you and the person you were photographing would be just a silhouette anyway. It's the same when looking at birds, especially through binoculars. I'll refer to this again as we have a quick look at different habitats.

RESERVOIRS AND GRAVEL PITS

Be careful to keep away from deep water, soft mud or collapsing banks. Ask permission, if necessary. Sometimes you may need a permit from the local water board, or fishing or yacht club. Get out early in the morning before the water sports start and scare all the birds away!

After a period of dry weather, a muddy or sandy shore may be exposed. This may attract waders, especially during spring and autumn. Even when there isn't a shoreline use your ears and listen out for the calls of birds flying over the reservoir. My reservoir in Birmingham had concrete banks and any wader trying to feed there would have bent its beak, but I DID see and hear lots of things flying over, especially early in the morning.

At the other end of the day, gulls often gather to roost on reservoirs. Learn to identify the different species and keep a record of the size of the flocks. It is often hard to actually count them all one by one. You can 'estimate' them by counting a group of say ten, 50 or even 100 and then going through the rest judging: 'well, there are eleven tens there, or twenty 300s.' (I will leave you to work out the totals as a quick maths lesson!)

In winter you'll find that there will be flocks of wildfowl to count too, although in summer many of these may disappear. This is because a lot of ducks actually come over to Britain from Europe during the harder weather. The few that do stay here to nest can become very secretive and hard to see during the breeding season.

Birds out in the middle of a stretch of water can be hard to identify. This is one of the situations where a telescope really can be useful. Also a walk round to the other side is worthwhile if it means getting that sun behind you; suddenly all those little black-looking ducks will burst into colour!

Many reservoirs and gravel pits have shallower bays, maybe just one end, or maybe even a smaller pool cut off from the main water by a road or causeway. These areas are often overgrown with reeds and willows. They are often excellent places to look for birds, including warblers on migration.

My own local patch: Brent reservoir, almost in the middle of London. If the wind is in the right direction, I can hear the crowds at Wembley Stadium!

17 MORE HABITATS

WOODS

Birdwatching amongst trees can be quite a challenge. The trick is to look for movement among the branches but this can be difficult when leaves are rustling and falling in the breeze. Remember though that leaves cannot fall UPWARDS! So learn to recognize the flick of wings. Find the sheltered side of the wood and, especially if it's the sunny side as well, that is where the flies will be buzzing and where the insect-eating birds will be feeding. Most of all, though, use your ears. If you can hear little birds squeaking but can't see them, try 'pishing'. Now I know this sounds really silly but what you do is make the sound 'pish pish pish' softly, or try kissing the back of your hand so it makes a kissy noise. Small birds, especially tits and Robins will come close to see what the noise is. We don't know why: maybe it sounds like an insect, another bird or a stoat or something, or maybe they are just

coming to laugh at you making silly noises! But it does work. Honestly. Try it.

It is definitely worth getting into the woods early, especially in spring, because that's when you'll hear the dawn chorus at its best. Try standing in the woods in May one morning just as it is getting light and try to recognize each species as it bursts into song. Even if you can't identify them all, the sound is simply wonderful.

ESTUARIES AND MARSHES

Many of the same rules (Whoops, I mean tips .. or should it be warnings?) apply to estuaries as to reservoirs. Beware of the mud, keep the sun behind you, get up early and so on. But there is also one other very important thing to take notice of on an estuary: the tide. An estuary can be pretty magical when the tide is low – miles and miles of lovely mud, with

Small woodland birds often flock together to 'mob' a Crow, Owl or bird of prey. Listen for their calls, follow the noise, and get a better look.

the distant calls of gulls and waders and maybe even wild geese in winter – but just try getting a decent view of anything! And on a hot autumn day it's even more difficult when everything shimmers in the heat haze. So, the golden rule (tip) for estuary watching is: check the tide tables (usually in the local newspaper). The best times to be at the estuary are just before or just after high tide. Actually AT high tide most waders stop feeding and gather together at a roost where they preen or have a snooze. These roosts are often way out on rocks or an island where you can't get at them. And anyway when they are all asleep with their heads tucked under their wings they are pretty hard to identify. So, find the last bit of mud to be covered before high tide or the first bit to be exposed after high tide, and that is where you'll see the birds.

There are of course masses of other habitats

A flock of waders going to roost. How many are there? Count a group of ten and then try to estimate the whole flock.

you can visit each with their special birds. Many of them are only at their best at certain times of the year and may be very quiet at others. For example, sea cliffs that are teeming with Guillemots, Razorbills and Puffins during the summer months are totally deserted for the rest of the year. On the other hand, farmland near the sea may have huge flocks of wild geese feeding on it in winter but nothing during the summer.

Generally it is fun to discover for yourself which places are good for birds, but now and again it is nice to make things easy by paying a visit to somewhere where you'll be more or less sure of seeing something good. Read on.

18 BIRD RESERVES

Most reserves are run by the RSPB or a local Trust for Nature. You may have to pay a small entrance fee if you are not a member. There are woodland, moorland, and sea bird reserves but what I am suggesting here is a visit to what I think is the most numerous kind of bird reserve: set on or near the coast, with marshes and possibly reed-beds and woodlands nearby. The chief attraction, though, will probably be shallow pools or 'scrapes' where waders and wildfowl flock together. Many of these may be driven off a nearby estuary by the high tide. So high tide is often the best time to visit a reserve.

The kiosk on the shore at Minsmere in Suffolk – probably the RSPB's most famous reserve.

There are lots of advantages in going to a bird reserve. For a start, everything is laid out so you see as much as possible and get the best possible views. There is usually an information centre that will tell you what's around that day and where you can buy everything from a cool drink to field guides, car stickers and Christmas cards. There will probably be plenty of other birdwatchers around too, so here is your chance to make friends and learn from the experts.

There will probably be several hides overlooking the reserve. They look a bit like enormous garden sheds. Hides are splendid but of course there are – you've guessed it – rules!

First of all, if there are hides on various sides of a large 'scrape' go into the one that ISN'T facing straight into the sun.

Second: don't make too much noise. There is usually a notice saying: 'Quiet please'. On the other hand, don't stop talking altogether. I'll tell you what I mean. It seems to me that often people get all embarrassed when they are lined up looking out of a hide. I think they are worried they might make a mistake and mis-identify a bird. So they go quiet. Or perhaps they are too shy to ask for help. Please don't be. You can bet that if you have seen something you cannot identify, there will be several other people in the hide who are just as puzzled. With a bit of luck, though, there will also be an experienced birdwatcher in there who will be only too willing to show off a bit by showing you the birds and telling you how to recognize them. So the rule here is: don't be afraid to ask.

Third: don't be afraid to make a mistake. If you spot what you think may be a rare bird, say so. It is perfectly possible that other people in the hide may not have even noticed it. If you are wrong, someone will explain why and you will have learned something. If you are right, they will be very grateful to you.

Another rule: take your time. I've seen people tumble into a hide ask 'anything about?' have one quick scan and race out again. Two minutes later something really rare has flown in. So stay there for at least half an hour and make sure you look carefully at ALL the birds on view. Not just the waders. There may be gulls and terns, a bird of prey may fly past and there'll be small birds skulking in the reeds. Birds come and go, so it is

Inside a hide at Titchwell on the north Norfolk coast. Plenty of telescopes to borrow!

worth just waiting there for a while. Especially if it looks like rain!

Finally, if you haven't got a telescope, don't be afraid to ask if you can look through someone else's (though it is best to make sure they are not trying to sort out some rarity at the time). If you have never looked through one before it may take you a minute or two to get used to it. It is worth it. I promise you will be thrilled by the extra special close-up view. The trouble is, you will probably go straight home and try to persuade your parents to buy you one for next birthday. Good luck.

This Titchwell hide is built right out into the marsh for extra close-up viewing.

19 MIGRATION

Migration is to me the most exciting thing about birds and birdwatching.

Many years ago some people used to believe that the reason swallows disappeared in the winter was that they flew off to the moon, whilst others believed that they hibernated under the sea. The truth is in fact even more amazing. What we mean when we say a bird is a migrant is fairly simple. It means that it spends its winter in the 'south' and then flies north to breed in summer. However, the journeys these migrants make are far from simple. Have a look at a globe or a map of the world. Across the other side of the Atlantic some birds breed way up in Arctic Alaska (found it) then fly down to South America for the winter. On the other side of the earth there are birds that breed in Siberia and winter in Australia. Closer to home 'our' migrants breed in northern Europe (including Britain) and fly south to Africa for our winter.

Many of these birds are very tiny – smaller than sparrows – and they do these journeys TWICE a year. They have no maps or compasses and – as far as we know – they can't ask the way. Even more amazingly many of them travel at night. The juveniles, born during a British summer, have never ever done the journey before. Neither do they travel with their parents. Now just think about that. Imagine your mum saying to you: 'right, you've got a long-lost cousin in South Africa. I don't know what his address is but I want you to go and visit him, but I can't afford to buy you any plane tickets, or maps, and I don't want you talking to any strange people. Oh, and I don't want you getting sunburned so you'd better travel in pitch darkness.' Do you reckon you would make it? Well the incredible thing is that every year millions and millions of small migrant birds DO make it. Swallows spend the winter in the company of the same herd of African elephants and then return to exactly the same beam in the same British barn to breed.

Scientists (ornithologists) have proved just how incredible these journeys are by putting little metal rings onto birds' legs. Each ring

Above The ring asks the finder to 'inform British Museum'. This one is big enough for a Swan.

Right This Sedge Warbler was ringed in Kent in September. Incredibly, the same British ringer then re-trapped it just after Christmas when he was on an expedition to Senegal, in West Africa!

The Arctic Tern is a record-breaking long distance migrant. Some Arctic Terns winter near the South Pole but breed near the North Pole. So every year their journeys are as far as flying round the earth.

has a number and an address on it so that if the bird is found or re-trapped it can be reported. In this way we learn how far and how quickly the birds can travel. Bird ringers have to be very carefully trained and it is not something that youngsters are allowed to do but if you ever visit a bird observatory where ringing is going on do ask if you can watch. Apart from anything else, it is wonderful to see birds in the hand. You will realize just how delicate they are and I am sure find it even more unbelievable that they can achieve their astonishing migrations.

How DO they find their way? Well it seems that night migrants are born with an ability to 'read' the patterns of the stars, and that they respond to the direction of the Sun and Moon and also the Earth's magnetic field. They may also use their calls to 'bounce' sound off the land or water below. And it seems that older birds do learn to recognize obvious 'landmarks' and may, for example, follow the lines of mountains or river valleys. But however they do it, be honest, it is a miracle!

A heligoland trap on Fair Isle. There are no trees or hedgerows on this remote northern isle, so small migrant birds are coaxed along stone walls into the 'catching boxes'.

20 STUDYING MIGRATION

Above Many British Starlings are migrants. These birds – feeding among Essex sheep in November – may well have just arrived from Russia.

Left Redwings are more often heard than seen.

The fact that birds do migrate explains why birdwatching is so exciting. Anything can turn up anywhere. You never know what you are going to see. If you watch your local patch regularly you will become aware of which birds are migrants and which are residents (the ones that don't leave the country in winter or summer). To me there is nothing more thrilling than actually seeing migration taking place. Spring and autumn are the most exciting times because that is when the birds are really on the move. Look out for them. If you watch a local reservoir or lake you will see the first swallows and martins skimming over the water in April and the nearby trees are suddenly alive with the songs of warblers: Chiffchaffs calling their names and Willow Warblers with their whispy little songs. A few days later they may nearly all seem to have gone. But they haven't left the country, they

have just spread out into the countryside where they will nest.

In autumn the swallows and martins will be gathering again, sometimes in huge roosts in the reed-beds and then lined up along the telephone wires before they suddenly all take to the air and head south. The trees by the reservoir will be full of warblers again but this time it will be young birds gobbling up insects which give them fuel for their long journey. By the time they arrive in Africa they will have flown across sea and desert and will be much thinner.

Then in late autumn the winter thrushes arrive. Some days you may see flocks of them but even more fascinating is to hear them passing over at night. Go outside just after dark in late October or early November (Bonfire Night is a good chance to try this) and listen. You may well hear little high-pitched squeaks.

Above You don't often see a single Fieldfare. There is usually a flock of them.

Left Five 'thrushes' in one picture: Redwing, Fieldfare, Blackbird, Song Thrush and Missel Thrush. I'll leave you to sort out which is which.

They are not bats. They are Redwings, which look rather like Song Thrushes but with a gleaming white eyebrow and an orangey underwing. Along with them you may hear 'chacks' and 'wheezes'. These are the calls of Fieldfares, another larger winter thrush. Both these species breed in Scandinavia and other parts of northern Europe but choose to fly south-west to Britain, where it is warmer, to spend the winter.

As well as the thrushes, you may hear other night migrants calling and sometimes you'll see them during the day, especially if you live near the coast or are watching an inland water. There may be flocks of Skylarks, Starlings, finches, pipits – all sorts of things – all purposefully migrating. The secret of observing them is to keep looking up and keep your ears open. And, like I said, absolutely anything can turn up.

Each year millions of migrants safely fly north or south. There are however, many that don't make it. Some will die for lack of food or water, others will be killed by natural predators like birds of prey. Tragically, many millions are also unnaturally slaughtered by hunters, especially in the countries round the Mediterranean.

There will also be some that get lost. We know that night migrants use the moon and stars to navigate partially because they are confused on dark foggy nights. They can be drawn to lighthouses like moths to a lamp and thousands can be grounded on the coast waiting for the weather to clear. Birds can also be blown off course by strong winds. Sometimes a bird can get VERY lost and end up a long way from home. A lost bird isn't necessarily a rare bird, but a rare bird IS definitely a lost bird. I shall explain.

21 RARE BIRDS

You may have seen photos in the paper of hundreds of birdwatchers who have travelled from all parts of the country just to see some rare bird. These birdwatchers are often called 'twitchers'. A twitcher spends most of his or her time chasing British rarities.

So what IS a British rarity? Well, it is a species that turns up in Britain let's say less than about twenty times a year. That would be worth chasing for most twitchers. The REAL rarities though are much rarer. Maybe they have been recorded less than twenty times in Britain, ever. And a really mega-rarity might be the first for this century or, best of all, a first time ever: a British first is every twitcher's dream.

As I said a rarity is lost. It has flown way off course, maybe blown by strong winds, or maybe it has just lost its sense of direction. It is perhaps not surprising that most rarities that turn up in autumn are young birds that are not as good at navigating as the adults. These mega-rarities can come a very long way. Each autumn westerly hurricanes blow birds right across the Atlantic, so that a little American wader or warbler ends up in Corn-

wall. In some winters Arctic birds wander much further south than usual, and now and again African birds fly far too far north. However, the majority of British rarities come from the east: the fairly rare ones from Scandinavia and the real mega-rarities from all the way across in Siberia!

As I hope I have already made clear, you cannot expect to see a rarity every time you go out birdwatching. And, as I hope I have also made clear, in fact it is just as exciting seeing new birds on your patch, or watching migration. However, I will admit that I LOVE finding rare birds. Notice I said 'finding'. That is not the same as going out and joining the twitchers watching something you already know is supposed to be there. You CAN do that (I will tell you how over the page). But for the moment let's suppose you want to increase your chances of finding a rarity yourself. First, you need to be at a likely place – which, inland, would be the reservoir or gravel pits or, on the coast, at a headland, estuary or marsh – at a likely time, which would be spring or autumn. Then, keep an eye on the weather, especially the wind direction. Remember I suggested that

A small flock of twitchers! A real mega rarity can attract a crowd of over a thousand. Too many for me!

Citrine Wagtail from Asia. One or two are recorded in Britain each year, usually in autumn, and once in summer.

Rustic Bunting. They breed in Northern Scandinavia, but this handsome male dropped down in Shetland for a day or two.

Black Winged Stilt. The most graceful of waders. Usually seen near the Mediterranean, but a pair bred in Norfolk a few years ago.

Crane. Bigger than a Heron, it is common in parts of Europe, but there are only six or so in Britain most years. It flies with its neck outstretched.

you noted the wind direction in your note book. This is why. A strong east wind, especially with some mist or rain is most likely to bring a rarity to the east coast or your reservoir. So that is when to get out there. If you are lucky enough to find something good, the fact that you can back up your description with the note 'strong east wind' will help your case, because it means a rarity is more likely. Never forget though that rarities ARE rare.

'Funny' looking birds are STILL more likely to be something common.

But you could get lucky. The best advice I can give if you do think you've found a rarity is to tell someone as quickly as possible. Don't worry that you might be wrong. Show an adult your notes and drawings and try and get them to see the bird. Many rarities have been found by youngsters and I'm sure many have been missed because adults took no notice!

22 AND THERE'S MORE

In a little book like this I can't possibly tell you everything about birdwatching. The great thing about it is that you can enjoy it in so many different ways. You can study your patch, or you can go twitching, or you might get into painting or photographing birds. You may want to become a serious ornithologist or a ringer or maybe you just want to stick at feeding the birds in the garden. Fair enough. It doesn't matter. It is all great fun. ENJOY it – that's the point.

JOINING THE CLUB

The one 'club' you really must join is the Royal Society for The Protection of Birds (RSPB). In fact you'd become a member of the Young Ornithologists Club. Please, please join. It's terrific value. You get a membership pack, a splendid magazine (*Bird Life*) six times a year and the chance to go on outings and meet other birdwatchers. What's more your membership fee goes to help save threatened habitats and birds. Write to, or call the RSPB (YOC) The Lodge, Sandy, Bedfordshire SG19 2DL, phone : 0767 680551

MORE READING

There are books about all aspects of birds and birdwatching. There are also magazines. As well as the YOC and RSPB magazines, it's well worth getting *Birdwatching* Magazine (monthly, from the newsagent), it has articles, adverts and excellent photos and illustrations. *Birdwatching* also has rare bird news, but if you want to be really up to date on rarities you need to call . . .

BIRDLINE

This is a phone number you can dial to find out the latest rare bird news from all over Britain. Each time you call, a charge is put on your phone bill, so I'm not going to give the number here or I could be in dead trouble with your parents! You'll find all the details in *Birdwatching*. If you do decide to use Birdline, please, you MUST tell mum or dad. And please don't call too often!

A last word from me on twitching. It really ISN'T the way to START birdwatching. It involves a lot of travelling and can be very expensive. What's more, I see too many young-sters these days who've got all sorts of rarities on their lists but don't know how to identify the common birds. You just don't NEED to twitch yet. Leave it as something to look forward to when you are old enough to drive!

AND NOT JUST BIRDS

I have to confess for years I went birdwatching but hardly noticed the wild flowers, butter-flies, trees and so on. Silly of me. For a start, it helps to find birds if you know the sort of trees and plants they prefer. What is more, a walk in the countryside (or indeed the town) is even more fascinating when you realize what a fantastic variety of wild and plant life there is to see. So, do get into all the other stuff as well. You couldn't do better than join your local WATCH group, organized by the Royal Society for Nature Conservation, The Green, Witham Park, Lincoln LN5 7JR, phone 0522 544400. Your school should know about them!